ZENDAYA

THERESE M. SHEA

PowerKiDS
press™

New York

Published in 2022 by The Rosen Publishing Group, Inc.
29 East 21st Street, New York, NY 10010

First Edition

Editor: Greg Roza
Designer: Rachel Rising

Photo Credits: Cover, p. 1 Albert L. Ortega/Contributor/Getty Images Entertainment/Getty Images; pp. 4, 6, 8, 10, 12, 14, 16, 18, 20, 21 Woskresenskiy/shutterstock.com; pp. 4, 6, 8, 10, 12, 14, 16, 18, 20, 21 Sunward Art/shutterstock.com; p. 5 Steven Ferdman/Stringer/Getty Images Entertainment/Getty Images; p. 7 Bill McCay/Contributor/WireImage/Getty Images; p. 9 Patrick McMullan/Contributor/Patrick McMullan/Getty Images; p. 11 Michael Buckner/Staff/Getty Images Entertainment/Getty Images; p. 13 Debra L Rothenberg/Contributor/Getty Images Entertainment/Getty Images; p. 15 Vincent Sandoval/Contributor/WireImage/Getty Images; p. 17 Robert Marquardt/Stringer/Getty Images Entertainment/Getty Images; p. 19 Lisa Maree Williams/Stringer/Getty Images Entertainment/Getty Images; p. 20 Michael Tran/Stringer/FilmMagic/Getty Images.

Library of Congress Cataloging-in-Publication Data

Names: Shea, Therese, author.
Title: Zendaya / Therese M. Shea.
Description: New York : PowerKids Press, [2022] | Series: African American
  superstars | Includes index.
Identifiers: LCCN 2020039475 | ISBN 9781725326231 (library binding) | ISBN
  9781725326217 (paperback) | ISBN 9781725326224 (6 pack)
Subjects: LCSH: Zendaya, 1996–Juvenile literature. | African American
  actors–Biography–Juvenile literature.
Classification: LCC PN2287.Z47 S53 2022 | DDC 791.4302/8092 [B]–dc23
LC record available at https://lccn.loc.gov/2020039475

Manufactured in the United States of America

CPSIA Compliance Information: Batch #CSPK22. For Further Information contact Rosen Publishing, New York, New York at 1-800-237-9932.

Find us on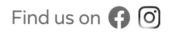

CONTENTS

Just Zendaya

Few actors go by one name. Zendaya is one who can. She first found fans through shows on the Disney Channel. However, she jumped to movies easily. Zendaya is known for her **fashion**. She also speaks out about **diversity** in Hollywood.

Her Name

Zendaya Maree Stoermer Coleman was born on September 1, 1996, in Oakland, California. Her parents, Claire and Kazembe, gave her an African first name. Zendaya means "to give thanks" in the language of the Shona people of Zimbabwe.

HAVEN
NIGHTCLUB

BOSTON

Young Actor

Zendaya's father worked for the California Shakespeare Theater. She grew up watching plays. She began acting at an early age. She studied dance too. She was a **model** and appeared on a **commercial**. Zendaya went to the Oakland School for the Arts.

Shake It Up

In 2010, Zendaya got her first big role, or part. She was 14 years old. She starred on a Disney TV show called *Shake It Up*. She and her co-star, Bella Thorne, sang and danced on the hit show.

11

Music and Dancing

In 2013, Zendaya was on the show *Dancing with the Stars*. She learned many kinds of dance for this **competition**. She and Val Chmerkovskiy placed second. Zendaya also released, or put out, her first music album in 2013.

13

K.C. Undercover

Zendaya's next Disney show was *K.C. Undercover*. She was 16. She played a spy named K.C. She asked to be a producer. That meant she could make **decisions** about the show. She made sure K.C.'s family was African American.

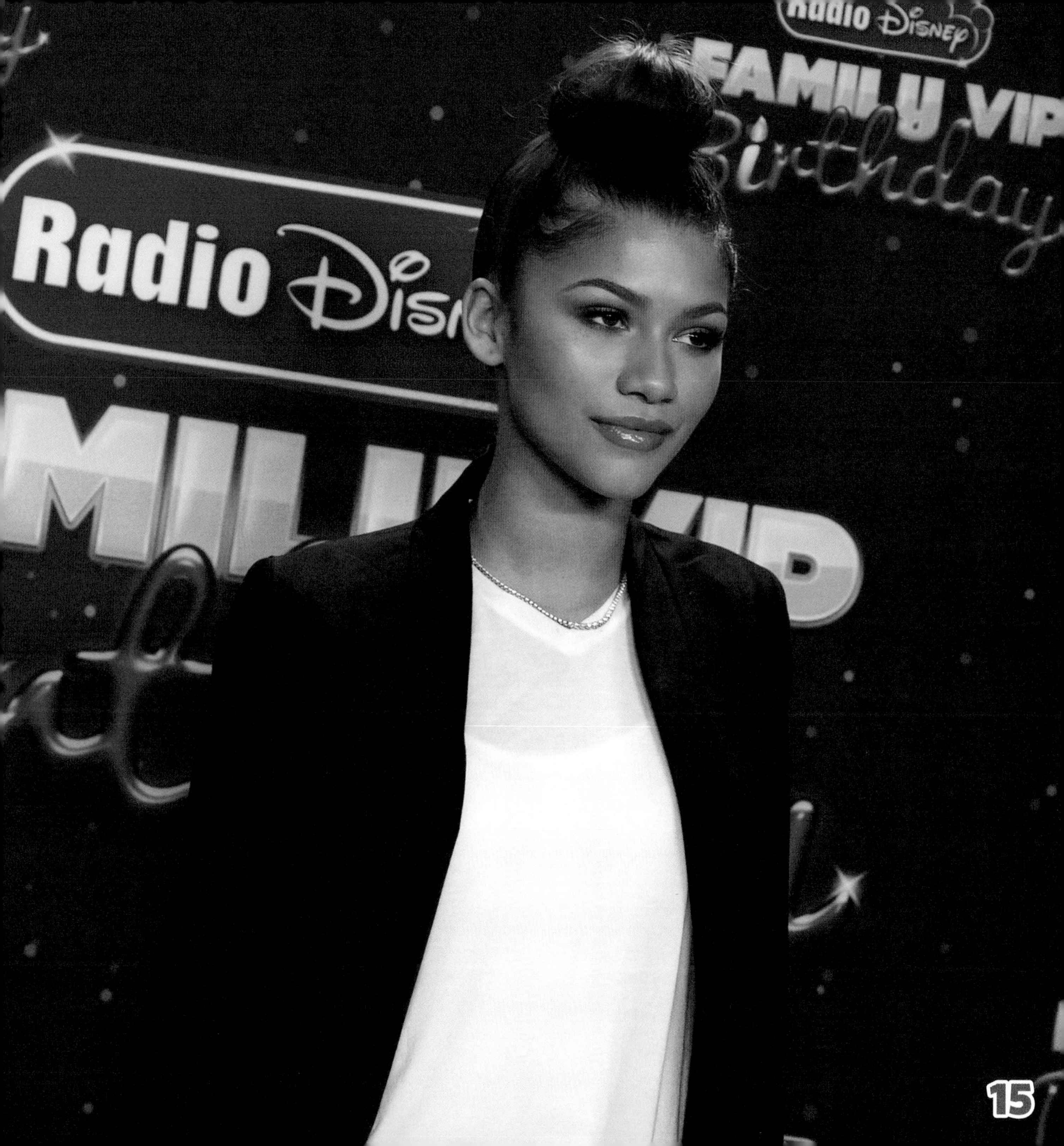
Radio Disney
FAMILY VIP
Birthday

As MJ

In 2017, Zendaya appeared in the hit movie *Spider-Man: Homecoming* as Michelle, or MJ. In 2019, Zendaya appeared as MJ again in a larger role in the movie *Spider-Man: Far from Home*. Zendaya liked that MJ was smart and "weird."

MARVEL STUDIOS
SPIDER-MAN
HOMECOMING
#SpiderManHomecoming

The Greatest Showman

In another 2017 movie, *The Greatest Showman*, Zendaya played a **trapeze** artist. She did most of her own **stunts**! She also sang some of the songs in the movie. She won some awards, or honors, for her role.

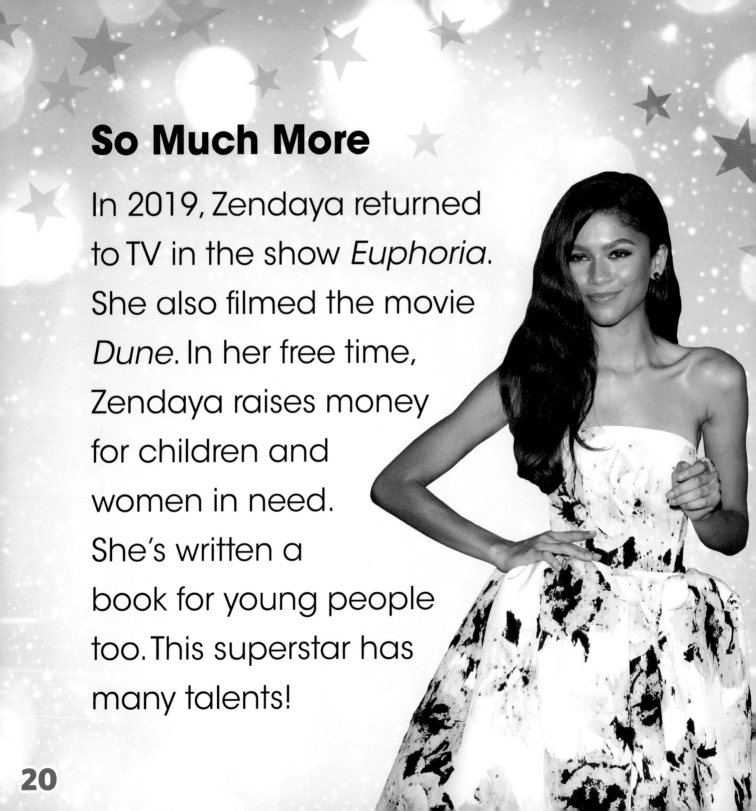

So Much More

In 2019, Zendaya returned to TV in the show *Euphoria*. She also filmed the movie *Dune*. In her free time, Zendaya raises money for children and women in need. She's written a book for young people too. This superstar has many talents!

TIMELINE

September 1, 1996	Zendaya is born in Oakland, California.
2010	She stars in *Shake It Up*.
2013	Zendaya releases a book called *Between U and Me: How to Rock Your Tween Years with Style and Confidence*.
2015	She plays a spy on *K.C. Undercover*. She is also a producer.
2017	Zendaya appears in the movies *Spider-Man: Homecoming* and *The Greatest Showman*.
2019	Zendaya stars in the show *Euphoria*.

GLOSSARY

commercial: A break during a TV show in which a company tries to sell something.

competition: An event in which people try to win or be the best at something.

decision: A choice made about something after thinking about it.

diversity: The state of having different races or cultures of people in a community.

fashion: Clothing styles or choices.

model: A person whose job is to show clothes or other things for sale.

stunt: An action or series of actions that is hard to do and is often dangerous.

trapeze: A bar hung high above the ground by two ropes that is held by performers who do tricks on it.

FOR MORE INFORMATION

BOOKS

Johnson, Robin. *Zendaya*. St. Catharines, ON, Canada: Crabtree Publishing, 2018.

Shea, Therese M. *Zendaya: Actress and Singer*. New York, NY: Enslow, 2019.

WEBSITES

Zendaya Biography
www.biography.com/actor/zendaya
Learn more about Zendaya and her amazing career at this thorough website.

Zendaya.com
zendaya.com
Stay up to date with Zendaya and her interests at her official website.

INDEX